SUCCESS

The 3 Insider Secrets

KA Man

DEDICATION

To Your Success

TABLE OF CONTENTS

ACKNOWLEDGMENTS

This book is made possible by the many successful people, educational books, and memorable events that have taught me the different secrets I am revealing here. The Subconscious Mind wanted me to share.

THE INTRODUCTION

Inspired by the Subconscious Mind, I wrote *Born to Create*. The short book is a collection of prose that explains why we must choose the inner journey to become the artist.

The creative journey involves risking our current life to pursue the one we are capable of. It includes finding our purpose. We all have one. It is our duty to find out what it is.

The joy is in discovering our true identity, finding meaning in our lives, and creating our art. The discovery leads to personal growth, happiness, and satisfaction. Any profits made because of the journey are purely unexpected bonuses.

After my profound experience which led to *Born to Create*, I am continuing on with this. In this short book, I am shifting focus away from our inner being and the powers beyond us to the strategic thinking and attitude of the artists who have struck financial gold.

There are various definitions of success. The successful in this book are defined as those who have attained worldly gains. They have maximised their time in this world to work on their profitable art.

While not all artists are guaranteed success, the successful people know how to create. The successful are the artists who have turned an intangible idea into a tangible and commercial enterprise.

They have showcased their art to the outside world and have not kept their art strictly for the pleasure of their souls. The price to pay for such a success is very high, but so is the reward.

The interpretation of art is not limited in structure or appearance. The art is not restricted to artistic endeavours like painting, but it covers other areas such as entrepreneurship.

Some artists have specific talents not in the artistic fields but in launching and running a profitable business. They find their purpose in building a product, a system, and a team.

Warren Buffett is a successful investor and a successful artist. He found his calling early in life, still enjoys his investing craft, and continues to work on his art - Berkshire Hathaway.

He is said to enjoy his craft so much that he "tap dances to work every morning". He has the extra satisfaction of performing very well. The consistent superior returns of Berkshire have made him among the richest people on this earth.

There are many successful artists who are not known to the public nor are associated with a specific sector as Buffett is in investing, or Beethoven is in creating music, or Van Gogh is in painting.

Their art only served a small community who are willing to pay. Their works not only delight their souls but also their bank accounts.

THE TWO WORLDS

We are not physical beings who have minds and spirits. Our bodies are not who we are. We are spirits and minds who live in physical bodies.

The physical body has limitation and does not stay the same. The body is susceptible to sickness, aging, and decay. Our spirit and minds have no limits.

Our minds live in two worlds. The first world is internal and has links to powers above us. The second world is where our physical bodies reside. This is the world where death, money, and time are real.

Humans have a better understanding of the second world and have created science around it.

Medical advancement has prolonged lives and has found cures for certain human ailments.

Industrial and technological discoveries have reduced costs, made us smarter and faster, and provided better connections.

The artist is a human who has captured an idea in the first world and brought it into the second. The art bridges the two worlds. The other creatures in this world do not have such abilities.

Our time in the second world is limited to one life. We can achieve only so much in one lifetime. We choose to either pursue our purpose or drift without one.

We will feel miserable and empty if we choose the latter. Those who do so often drown their sorrows with distractions and pleasures of the body that do not last.

It is the combined pleasures of the mind and the soul that has permanence.

The spirit seeks growth and wants us to reach our full potential. But, our past narrative brings doubts into our mind and reminds us our bodies have many limitations.

As the mind is the connector to the other realm, it has powerful guards to defend against negativity. The guards will only awake when the power source is strong and active.

THE POWER SOURCE

While we cannot deny that all accomplished people have the good fortune of being at the right place at the right time and knowing the right people, there are other factors in play.

We will focus on the first of three elements they are in control of and not those of chance or circumstances.

The first common characteristic among the accomplished artist is a strong mindset. This is the foundation of success.

Think of success as the delicious fruits of a strong tree. The strong roots are the foundation. We need a strong foundation to build and grow anything. Otherwise, whatever that is built on the weak foundation will crumble and there are no fruits to savour.

A strong mindset is needed to become the artist as the creative journey is an internal challenge. A strong mindset is a strict requirement when the art is also exposed in public and competition in the free market is fierce.

Focus is becoming a rare attribute because we are living in a world where there is an increasing demand for our consideration and our capacity.

The information and requests coming at us are speeding up because of technological advancements. But the human body needs space, rest, and recovery to operate effectively and efficiently.

Being able to focus is crucial in these times as the less important tasks are always seeking our attention. We may want to do everything but that is not possible. If we try, we may end up doing nothing important.

Singularity of focus allows the use of all their brain power on one essential task and not get sidetracked by the much lower priorities.

The successful focus on developing and being their true selves. The concentration is on what truly matters as opposed to the noise. The material gains come when the art is needed and valued.

Being bold in the modern day differs from the times of our ancestors. Having courage is no longer about facing predators that threaten our survival.

In modern society, having courage is to face our inner demons, and that is not lethal. We can conquer fear if we make up our minds to do so as fear exists nowhere except in our minds.

Practice the breathing exercise when there is fear lurking around. Breathe in and keep courage. Breathe out and release fear.

We do not need to fight the old narrative but the courage to take over and start anew. The past is over, be mindful of the present. There is a reason why the present is a present. It is a beautiful gift.

Being bold is to have a big vision, audacious goals, and the guts to take massive actions. The successful are committed and have a realistic attitude toward putting in the hard work and have strong work ethics.

They often have a dark past. This drives them towards the vision, instead of pulling them away. They execute their visions ferociously and quickly.

They are unafraid to take on the risk as long as the risk is not fatal, or may wipe them financially.

A lion does not find the hunt for a mouse challenging. Reward requires risk. The hunt for the antelope has a risk. It has horns. But its meat will satisfy the lion's hunger and sustain its energy.

The successful artists have taken the chance and entered the ring. They have figured out the price and have paid. They become the players who take part in the game and not the spectators who watch.

They have learned that challenges are often not as scary as they appear. The accomplished have the confidence to figure out a solution and the trust it will work out fine.

They understand that what seems unattainable and seems over their depth is based on what they understand at a point. It does not stay that way once they start.

It is the strength to start, and not the intelligence, that makes the difference. They often say yes to the opportunities and then find out a way to make it happen.

It doesn't matter where they are starting from. Once they made the leap, the net will appear. They will learn what they never knew as they move along. The path they never saw before will gradually emerge.

The successful artists take responsibility and accepts full accountability for all that happens; the good, bad, and the ugly. There is no blame, denial, or excuses. It is about winning, not whining.

They are resilient and do not let failures stop them from finishing their art. Resilience is the ability to recover from serious setbacks. The strength of resilience is measured by how quick they spring back after a serious loss.

There are lots of challenges on the road to completing a great art. The successful fail their way forward to success. It is never about the falling, but the rising and moving forward after the fall.

They will regularly fall but they don't stay down for long. They may encounter many defeats but these do not defeat them. The wounds of adversity do not stick on them.

The successful can tackle tough conditions and find solutions to overcome them. They have recognised that it is pressure that builds the diamonds inside.

Mastering hardship brings confidence, contentment, and growth. Strength only comes after the struggle. The successful use these failures to strengthen the muscles to push forward their progress.

They know bigger adversities bring bigger rewards. It is in the darkest of times, they find out their true selves. That alone is a big enough reward, but there are more.

They are comfortable with change so any unexpected changes do not rattle them. They are confident of being able to adapt to any changes.

They have grown accustomed with constant pain of progress. They do not let the pain of failure get into their hearts as they do not let the vindication of success get into their heads.

The accomplished know their choices made at painful moments determine the quality of their lives. As they grow fast, they will break through the limits. Breaking through can be excruciating.

The higher the artists are on the success ladder, the more and bigger are the problems they face. The intensity of the problems does not reduce but increases. This is not an issue as their ability to handle these problems has risen as well.

It is always crowded where there are little adversities. When the successful artists find themselves in a crowd, they pause and question whether their ladder is leaning on the right building.

The accomplished are optimists at heart. They know the challenging situation will become right so they are willing to make the medium-term sacrifices.

The successful have acquired the ability to delay gratification. They know there is a price to pay, either now or later. The investment is cheaper now than later. The future will eventually become the present. Investment is not always about money.

They have developed a firm control of their emotions. They deal only with the emotion that serves their purpose.

They do not want to deal with a bunch of volatile damaging emotions. With their emotions in check, they can think objectively and focus intensely.

Harmful emotions are the biggest threat to good decisions. Bad emotions forces impulsive actions that cause remorse later. The successful stay far away from gossips, politics, and drama.

Their attitude helps them handle pressure well. When the situation goes wrong, they remain calm and able to think clearly. These attributes make them good decisive decision makers.

The successful are independent thinkers who do not mind being wrong. They make contrarian bets. More often than not, they are right. They will bet big if they are convinced that the payoff is huge, and the risk is worth it.

Warren Buffett made his best and boldest investments during the crisis that rocked the companies he is interested in. His faith and ability to think through the chaotic situations made him rich.

The accomplished loathe making many unimportant daily decisions. They adopt a simple lifestyle and habits so the only decisions they make are the major ones that matter. They want the mental space to think deeply about the critical decisions.

Habits keep them moving when the motivation is gone. Motivation is only needed to start, but it does not stay for long. Good habits make the soul happy. Good habits also make the heart, body, and mind healthy.

Their daily activities of the successful are rarely exciting. They have boring schedules most of the time. But they are happy to lead this kind of lifestyle.

They make good health a priority. They are careful about what they eat and exercise regularly. A healthy body is needed for optimal mental performance and relates to time and energy. Learning is also a priority. They often apply what they learn. They spent time to reflect on the feedback received. This learning process allows them to grow inside.

KA MAN

THE SACRED RESOURCE

Time only exists in the material world. Therefore, time has relevance only for those wishing material success. The successful understand the importance of focus and plan to get the most of their limited time on earth.

We are protective of our money because we easily recognise its value. We see the value printed on the currency. We use our money to exchange for goods and services. We want more of it to buy stuff and experiences, and for security.

However, most of us do not recognise the true value of our time. Most think the value of our time is based on what we are paid at our jobs. We calculate what we earn per hour by dividing our annual salary to the total hours worked in a year.

We value money and time differently depending on the stage we are in life. The relative importance of money and time changes as we grow older. It is also based on our financial situation at a certain point in time. What we overlook, we later hold dearly.

When we were young, we have spent time like water because we think we have lots of it and it is free. We spare no thought of the future. We spent our youth chasing money.

When we are old, we may have the money. But we have little time left, so we treasure every moment. If illness strikes, we spend much money to prolong time.

The same concept applies to those who are in different financial positions. Those who are struggling are naturally focused on making money so they happily exchange time for money.

Those who are successful focus on their quality of time as money is no longer an issue. The higher the achievements, the bigger the premium is placed on time.

Born to Create goes in depth about the true value of our time. Its true value is in finding meaning in our lives and creating our art. The successful artist has taken a step further.

They enjoy the benefits of living out their lives purposefully while making a good living and making a positive impact among their community. They go to bed knowing they have made progress on creating something wonderful for the world.

We all have the same amount of time, 24 hours or 1,440 minutes in a day. Yet, the successful do more, achieve more, and earn more compared to the others. There is a secret to why this is so.

No one owns time although we can spend it. No one can store this irreplaceable resource although we can use it. Once time is gone, no one gets it back.

When we run out of money, we can borrow or look for ways to earn more money. When we run out of time, we are dead. Death has a nasty habit of not calling first before it visits.

SUCCESS

We do not know how much time we have remaining. We must fulfil our aspirations within the time we have left and not beg for more time to prove ourselves when it is too late.

Their secret is they strategically plan out the use of their time. They set schedules with time blocks for their main priorities. They do not allow distractions in during these periods.

They recognise that not all things matter equally. Some are vital while the majority are not. The successful use much of their time on what truly matters. They never let the unimportant affect the important.

They know that the better use of their time improves the quality of lives including their own. They invest their time. They create value and solutions. Meanwhile, the others spend their time consuming and reacting to external events.

The successful have come to realised that they must manage their thoughts to manage their time. The mind has a strong influence on the quality of time.

When the mind is distracted, time is wasted as the artist is not able to focus attention and energy on producing good art.

Their early mornings are often their cherished moments in the day. This is when their creative energy is at its highest. They know they can control only the quality of the energy and not the number of hours in a day.

The successful are proactive in the morning. They know it is difficult to revert to being proactive after starting the day being reactive. It is much easier the other way around.

Being proactive is doing the difficult task that involves critical thinking. Reactive is being busy with stimulating and easy work such as watching television, checking email, and social media.

They are vigilant about defending their non-renewable resource, time. They are careful about how they exchange this necessary resource; that which they have little to give away each day.

Everything takes our time. Every activity occurs in time and uses it up. Everything we do has an opportunity cost. The time we spent on one task robs us of time to do another.

The word "No" is a regularly used word among those who are successful. They are so comfortable using the word to the extent of liking it. The successful are often not accessible and they make no apology for that.

There was an infinite amount of money in the global system before the Financial Crisis of 2008. Large sums of money were printed and added to the monetary system after the crisis.

This additional liquidity has flowed into global assets and created a financial boom in stocks, start-ups, and real estate. This boom has made the billionaire club no longer exclusive.

But there is a finite amount of time in a lifespan. No human, corporation, or government has the power to create time. The clock starts ticking the day we are born. This is the reality of our time clock.

While there is a bountiful supply of money circulating the globe, there is also ample amount of needs and wants. The successful are the ones able to provide for these needs and wants.

The size of their income is tied to their ability to address the intensity, size, and urgency of the need of a marketplace.

With time being a more valuable asset than money, they place a higher value on how they invest their time compared to how they invest their money. Their key measurement is the return of their time.

They rather save time than money. They are fine losing their money if their investments have poor returns but have little patience if their time is spent poorly.

When they evaluate a project, they focus on the impact of the project, the time needed, and whether they can leverage the outcome.

KA MAN

THE POWER LEVER

Behind every successful artist is a person who has mastered the ability to use their mind and their time effectively.

The power of leverage helps them save time, effort, and attention while it magnifies their returns. Leverage makes lives better, makes work easier, and produces results faster.

The successful are masters at the leverage game. They use the Pareto principle by concentrating their efforts on the 20% that brings about 80% of the results. Some even go further by concentrating their efforts on the 20% of the 20%.

They appreciate the need to scale over what they can do to become outstanding. They employ the services of other humans, machines, and tools.

The successful understand the best value of money is to buy time. They use money to multiply themselves.

They will spend thousands of dollars to get a mentor and expert advice as this saves them time and fast track their progress. They rather pay money than pay in time to learn.

They will pay tens of dollars for someone to run their errands, do their shopping, and clean their homes. They outsource their chores and tasks to others so they don't have to do them.

They leverage capital by borrowing to buy and expand their business or estate. They are aware that savings is slow and is a difficult way to raise capital.

The successful are clear what good borrowings is and what it is not. The good debt improves their returns despite the interest costs. Their returns of good debt are not restricted to financial matters.

Warren Buffett is an example of a leverage master. He leverages his learnings from his mentorship with Benjamin Graham and his partnership with Charlie Munger.

He leverages the float from his insurance companies to obtain cheap cost of funds to invest. He leverages on his connections, emotions, and intelligence to take advantage of market opportunities when they arise.

He leverages on his credibility and his war chest to take up significant stakes in privately held companies. He leverages the compound returns over a few decades to build financial wealth.

THE INCOMPLETE SUCCESS

The successful artist is paid well to do the meaningful. This should be a winning life formula but not all artists who have achieved are completely satisfied.

This is baffling but there are explanations to this mystery. The main ones are centred on gratitude, recovery, external influence, comparison, contribution, and the need for a new direction.

These unhappy artists have taken for granted how much they have evolved. They have forgotten their tough battles fought to bring the many good things in their lives.

These unhappy artists have not celebrated their success and taken time off to recuperate. They suffer burnout because they have not maintained a long-term lifestyle balance.

These unhappy artists created their art driven more by external motives than the inner calling. Achieving external success without fully satisfying the soul leaves the achiever incomplete and lack lasting happiness.

These unhappy artists compare themselves to others instead of comparing themselves to the past. They neglect counting the blessings of which they have plenty but on the misses which they have a few. Happiness is to never compare.

They have forgotten to give back. The contribution is more important for the giver than the receiver. The happiest in life are the givers, not the receivers. It is therefore not a coincidence that the biggest contributors to our society are also the richest.

The self-made has found meaning in the sector they operate in. Once they become dominant in this arena and their financial comfort is met, they often need to find a new direction. Many retire into philanthropy searching for a new path by helping others.

THE LEGACY SECRET

The successful have asked, and they are given abundantly. To whom much is given, much is expected. They have honoured the gifts given by being the best they can be.

Many of the successful are aware that their fame, power, and possessions are not theirs to keep. These are merely loans they must pay back when they return their physical bodies.

They are responsible to return these loans with substantial interest. The amount they repay signifies how well they employed themselves and the success they have achieved.

Andrew Carnegie is said to have grown his starting net worth of almost nothing to $309 billion (by today's standard). His major goal was to spend the first half of his life accumulating money and the second half to giving it all away.

But he failed meeting his second half objective when he passed on. However, there is a lesser-known billionaire who succeeded where Carnegie failed.

The late Chuck Feeney quietly gave away over $8 billion. The founder of Duty Free Shoppers may be the first billionaire to give all while he was still alive.

He did not have a building, a library, or a statue named to honour his contributions but he left a legacy. He inspired other wealthy individuals, including Warren Buffett, to give away a large part of their wealth to charitable causes.

KA MAN

THE CONCLUSION

We were not born to die; we were born to create. We need to create our story and find our inner voice before our existence end in ashes. Use death to inspire us and not waste any more precious time. In the process of creating, we find meaning in our lives and find our true identity. Happiness is to create.

Once we have completed our art, we change the trajectory of our lives for the better. We have witnessed the powers beyond comprehension. We are uniquely qualified to be ourselves. We will never go back to our old selves.

We are all capable of becoming the artist. It is our right, our privilege, and our destiny. It is also our choice. We can choose the easy now but pay later option, or we can choose the difficult one and discover powers not obvious to the eyes.

We were not born as a successful artist but we can strive to become a successful one. Desiring to be the best is the starting point of success.

Wanting the best will make us work towards providing value to others. We can only help others after we have helped ourselves. Those who have most money can give the most money.

Do not mistake that wanting the best to wanting perfection. The very successful artist is not a perfect being. There is no perfect human. We are all flawed in different areas.

We are all multidimensional. We often categorise ourselves in black or white. But the fact is that we are all grey.

We are strong in one aspect and weak in another. The successful artists are likely to overcompensate in one area at the expense of another.

The successful artist is strong in the area that has a meaning and has little care of the areas that are not.

It is about being the best version of ourselves. If this includes being successful, all the better as we can serve others too.

Success boils down to two crucial elements, mindset and time. Mindset being the foundation and time being the space to build the foundation. Behind every overnight success is a strong foundation built over time.

We think the secret to becoming successful is having the right knowledge, talents, and skills. The truth is 75% of success is getting the mind optimised. The successful leverage most of the other 25%.

Every day, people are becoming the artist. Some artists go on to become successful. Stop hoping for the purpose to drop by or wishing for success. Go find them.

SUCCESS

THANK YOU FOR READING

I truly hope the content in this book speaks to you and opens up wonderful possibilities.

If you have enjoyed reading this book, please leave a review on Amazon and share on social media.

With gratitude,
KA Man

ABOUT THE AUTHOR

KA Man is the author of Born to Create. He can be contacted at Kaman@whoiskaman.com. His website is www.whoiskaman.com